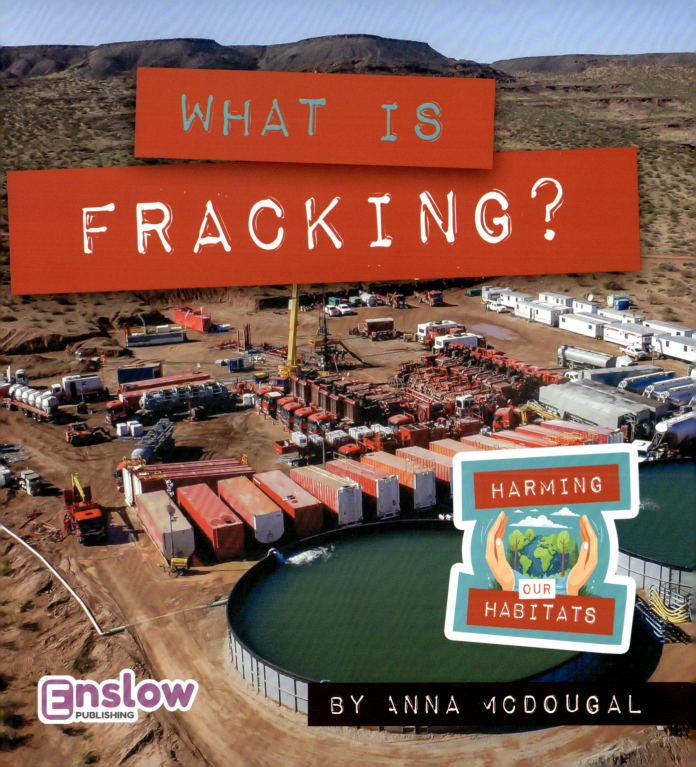

Please visit our website, www.enslow.com. For a free color catalog of all our high-quality books, call toll free 1-800-398-2504 or fax 1-877-980-4454.

Library of Congress Cataloging-in-Publication Data
Names: McDougal, Anna, author.
Title: What is fracking? / Anna McDougal.
Description: Buffalo, NY : Enslow Publishing, [2026] | Series: Harming our habitats | Includes bibliographical references and index.
Identifiers: LCCN 2024043438 (print) | LCCN 2024043439 (ebook) | ISBN 9781978543393 (library binding) | ISBN 9781978543386 (paperback) | ISBN 9781978543409 (ebook)
Subjects: LCSH: Hydraulic fracturing–Juvenile literature. | Gas industry–Environmental aspects–Juvenile literature.
Classification: LCC TN871.255 .M385 2026 (print) | LCC TN871.255 (ebook) | DDC 622/.3381–dc23/eng/20241214
LC record available at https://lccn.loc.gov/2024043438
LC ebook record available at https://lccn.loc.gov/2024043439

Published in 2026 by
Enslow Publishing
2544 Clinton Street
Buffalo, NY 14224

Copyright © 2026 Enslow Publishing

Portions of this work were originally authored by Ryan Nagelhout and published as *Fracking*. All new material in this edition is authored by Anna McDougal.

Designer: Leslie Taylor
Editor: Caitlin McAneney

Photo credits: Cover (photo) Sobrevolando Patagonia/Shutterstock.com; Series Art (HOH logo) AI Generated art/Shutterstock.com; Series Art (peach shape) chyworks/Shutterstock.com; Series Art interior (planet earth) Y Salnikova/Shutterstock.com; Series Art (background earth/sky) Background Land/Shutterstock.com; p. 5 Janice Chen/Shutterstock.com; p. 7 juninatt/Shutterstock.com; p. 8 George Sheldon/Shutterstock.com; p. 9 Margaret M Stewart/Shutterstock.com; p. 11 drnadig/Shutterstock.com; p. 13 VectorMine/Shutterstock.com; p. 15 Viktor Osipenko/Shutterstock.com; p. 17 Aleksa Georg/Shutterstock.com; p. 19 Edgar G Biehle/Shutterstock.com; p. 21 Irina Wilhauk/Shutterstock.com.

All rights reserved. No part of this book may be reproduced in any form without permission in writing from the publisher, except by a reviewer.

Some of the images in this book illustrate individuals who are models. The depictions do not imply actual situations or events.

Printed in China

CPSIA compliance information: Batch #QSENS26. For further information contact Enslow Publishing at 1-800-398-2504.

CONTENTS

We've Got the Power 4
Fracking Facts 6
America Faces Fracking 8
Waste Left Behind 10
What's in That Water? 12
That's Toxic! 14
Wild Animals in Danger 16
Harming Humans 18
What's Right? 20
Glossary 22
For More Information 23
Index 24

Words in the glossary appear in **bold** type the first time they are used in the text.

WE'VE GOT THE POWER

What powers your home, your car, or the airplanes in the sky? Most things we use run on **fossil fuels**, including natural gas. Fossil fuels are **nonrenewable resources**, so we risk running out of them someday. Also, habitats face the fallout from our use of fossil fuels.

THINK ABOUT IT!

Fracking is the practice of hydraulic fracturing. This practice forces natural gas from deep underground using strong blasts of water.

Habitats are the natural homes of animals, which have everything they need to survive. If habitats are lost or harmed, animals—and people—suffer.

Burning fossil fuels pollutes the air. Burning natural gas is a bit cleaner for the **environment** than oil or coal. However, the way we get natural gas from the earth—sometimes by fracking—can harm habitats.

FRACKING FACTS

What is fracking anyway? First, a well is drilled down into a layer of **sedimentary rock** called shale. Then, the drill is turned, and a tunnel is made side-to-side through the shale. Next, a mix of water, sand, and chemicals is pumped through the tunnel at high speed. This cracks, or fractures, the shale, freeing the natural gas to flow to the surface.

Fracking pollutes the air, water, and land. It uses millions of gallons of water per well, as well as harmful chemicals.

Shale is a rock made after mud faces great pressure and heat over a long period of time.

THINK ABOUT IT!

More than 43 percent of energy use in the United States is from natural gas.

7

AMERICA FACES FRACKING

Fracking is a growing **industry** in the United States. More than 30 states practice fracking. It's big business in places like Texas and Pennsylvania.

A huge amount of natural gas is found in the Marcellus Shale, an area of sedimentary rock which stretches across New York and into Pennsylvania and West Virginia.

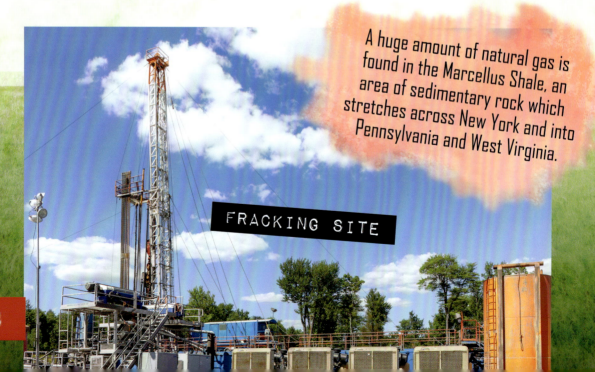

FRACKING SITE

SHALE

Shale plays are areas where natural gas is found. They're found all over the United States. Energy companies think natural gas from these shale plays is useful. They say it will decrease the country's **dependence** on fossil fuels from overseas. Some people want to grow fracking to give us "cleaner" energy. Others worry about fracking's harmful effects.

THINK ABOUT IT!

Some states, including Vermont and Washington, have banned fracking. That means it's unlawful to drill for natural gas. Why do you think fracking was banned in these states?

WASTE LEFT BEHIND

Drilling for natural gas leaves behind a lot of harmful waste. Fracking fluid is filled with **toxic** chemicals, some of which can cause **cancer**.

Much of the fracking solution comes back to the surface. It is then called brine, wastewater, or flowback. It's full of salt, chemicals, and harmful metals from deep within Earth. Some fracking wastewater is stored in human-made ponds or underground. It is sometimes reused or treated to make it clean again.

Fracking waste can include harmful metals such as radium, uranium, and lead.

THINK ABOUT IT!

Frack ponds are meant to keep fracking waste away from habitats. What are some challenges in keeping waste separate from groundwater and soil?

WHAT'S IN THAT WATER?

Unfortunately, toxic fracking wastewater isn't always kept separate from habitats. Spills are a regular problem at frack ponds. The pipes leading from wells to ponds crack and leak wastewater into the ground. Animals may drink the toxic puddles. Fracking fluid or flowback can also get into water supplies when spilled or dumped into rivers and streams, killing fish.

THINK ABOUT IT!

Fracking wells often go through aquifers, or places where groundwater can be found. Wastewater may reach the aquifers and make its way into the water supply.

HOW FRACKING WORKS

STORAGE TANKS

DRILLING WELL

PRIVATE WELL

AQUIFER / DRINKING WATER

FRACKING ZONE

Check out how close fracking happens to the aquifer and water supply.

The amount of water it takes for fracking to happen is also a problem. Fresh water is taken from the habitats that need it.

13

THAT'S TOXIC!

Accidents happen. Fracking fluid may enter the water supply even if companies are trying to be safe. People who live nearby often aren't told about it. They may get sick because of the toxic chemicals in the water.

Where fracking occurs, animals around the drill **sites** may go from healthy to very ill. Some pet owners and farmers have claimed their animals died because of fracking. Some tests have found heavy metals and toxic matter in their bodies.

Scientists are studying the effects of fracking on farm animals. Baby animals born near fracking sites sometimes have health issues.

THINK ABOUT IT!

If animals who die from poisoning are eaten, those toxins may enter the food supply. How do you think that could affect the food people eat?

WILD ANIMALS IN DANGER

Wild animals need their habitats to survive. Some animals are already endangered, or in danger of dying out. Environmental activists worry that fracking can harm the populations of endangered species. Some may die from toxic wastewater, while others have their habitats polluted or used for drill sites.

THINK ABOUT IT!

Fish in streams near fracking sites have been found dead. How might this affect the natural food chain in a habitat?

The California condor is an endangered bird that could suffer from habitat loss and pollution due to fracking in California.

Building fracking wells means big trucks need to reach remote places. However, these roads run through wild habitats. They can break up land, making it hard for animals to find a home and food.

HARMING HUMANS

Animals aren't the only ones who suffer. Some fracking sites are in areas far from homes—others are nearby. There are many stories about people becoming ill living near fracking sites. Some people become dizzy, out of breath, or very sick.

Fracking can also bring methane into new areas. This harmful gas is bad for health. It also makes **climate change** worse. Climate change causes warmer temperatures and worse storms, which can be very harmful.

Some people allow fracking near their homes without knowing how it can affect their health.

THINK ABOUT IT!

Fracking can even cause seismic activity, or little earthquakes. How might this affect people's homes?

19

WHAT'S RIGHT?

Some people argue that fracking allows us to get to fuel that is cleaner than burning other fossil fuels. They point out that many fracking companies try to keep waste safely **contained**. Some send brine to be treated so they don't use as much water.

THINK ABOUT IT!

Laws have been passed on the state level to limit fracking in some places. How do you think laws can help keep the environment safe?

Kids can help! You can write letters to leaders about local habitats. You can speak out about fracking if you think it is more harmful than helpful.

On the other hand, fracking has serious effects on the environment. Some companies don't properly contain or reuse waste. People and animals have gotten sick from fracking sites. What do you think? Is fracking worth the harm it brings?

GLOSSARY

cancer: A disease caused by the uncontrolled growth of cells in the body.

climate change: Long-term change in Earth's climate, caused mainly by human activities such as burning oil and natural gas.

contain: To hold something in.

dependence: The condition of relying on something.

environment: The conditions that surround a living thing and affect the way it lives.

food chain: A series of organisms in which one uses the next lowest one as food.

fossil fuel: Matter formed over millions of years from plant and animal remains that is burned for power.

industry: A group of businesses that produce a product.

nonrenewable resource: Something that is used which, once it has been used, is not replaceable.

sedimentary rock: The rock that forms when sand, stones, and other matter are pressed together over a long time.

site: A place where something happens.

toxic: Containing poison.

FOR MORE INFORMATION

Books

Andrews, E. C. *Water Pollution*. Buffalo, NY: PowerKids Press, 2025.

Ting, Jasmine. *Green Energy*. New York, NY: Children's Press, 2024.

Websites

Freshwater Habitat
kids.nationalgeographic.com/nature/habitats/article/freshwater
Learn more about freshwater habitats and the animals that call them home.

Clean Energy for Kids
energync.org/forkids/
Discover interesting facts about clean energy with the North Carolina Sustainable Energy Association.

Publisher's note to educators and parents: Our editors have carefully reviewed these websites to ensure that they are suitable for students. Many websites change frequently, however, and we cannot guarantee that a site's future contents will continue to meet our high standards of quality and educational value. Be advised that students should be closely supervised whenever they access the internet.

INDEX

animal health, 14, 15, 21

climate change, 18

endangered species, 16, 17

fossil fuels, 4, 5, 9, 20

fracking bans/limits, 9, 20

frack ponds, 10, 11, 12

habitats, 4, 5, 11, 12, 16, 17, 21

human health, 10, 18, 19

Marcellus Shale, 8

methane, 18

natural gas, 4, 5, 6, 7, 8, 9, 10

Pennsylvania, 8

pollution, 5, 6, 16, 17

shale, 6, 7, 9

Texas, 8

Vermont, 9

Washington, 9

wastewater, 10, 12, 16, 20

water, 4, 6, 11, 12, 13, 14, 20